Amelia Earhart

by Lola M. Schaefer

Consulting Editor: Gail Saunders-Smith, Ph.D.
Consultants: Mike Jackson, Executive Director
Tara Engel, Research Center Director
National Aviation Hall of Fame
Dayton, Ohio

Pebble Books

an imprint of Capstone Press
Mankato, Minnesota

Pebble Books are published by Capstone Press
151 Good Counsel Drive, P.O. Box 669, Mankato, Minnesota 56002
http://www.capstone-press.com

1 2 3 4 5 6 07 06 05 04 03 02

Library of Congress Cataloging-in-Publication Data
Schaefer, Lola M., 1950–
    Amelia Earhart / by Lola M. Schaefer.
    p. cm.—(First biographies)
    Summary: A brief biography of the first woman pilot to cross the Atlantic Ocean
and to fly alone across the United States, as well as the first pilot to fly alone across
the Pacific Ocean.
    Includes bibliographical references and index.
    ISBN 0-7368-1433-7 (hardcover)
    ISBN 0-7368-9408-X (paperback)
    1. Earhart, Amelia, 1897–1937—Juvenile literature. 2. Air pilots—United States—
Biography—Juvenile literature. [1. Earhart, Amelia, 1897–1937. 2. Air pilots.
3. Women—Biography.] I. Title. II. Series.
TL540.E3 S33 2003
629.13'092—dc21   2002001210

Note to Parents and Teachers

The First Biographies series supports national history standards for units on people and culture. This book describes and illustrates the life of Amelia Earhart. The images support early readers in understanding the text. This book also introduces early readers to subject-specific vocabulary words, which are defined in the Words to Know section. Early readers may need assistance to read some words and to use the Table of Contents, Words to Know, Read More, Internet Sites, and Index/Word List sections of the book.

Table of Contents

Time Line

1897
born

Amelia Earhart was born in Kansas in 1897. Amelia and her sister sometimes lived with their grandparents.

Amelia (right) and sister Murial Earhart

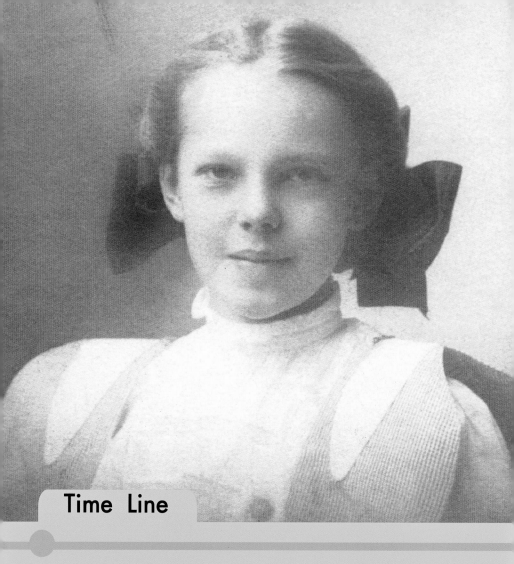

Time Line

1897
born

Amelia loved to learn and explore. She and her sister played games outdoors. They pretended to travel to faraway places.

Amelia at about age 10

Time Line

1897
born

1917
works in
hospital

Amelia worked as a nurses' helper in a hospital during World War I. She met pilots and visited airfields. Amelia liked airplanes.

Amelia as a nurses' helper

Time Line

| 1897 born | 1917 works in hospital | 1920 takes first airplane ride |

In 1920, Amelia went to an air show in California. She rode in an airplane for the first time. Amelia loved flying. She took flying lessons.

Time Line

1897
born

1917
works in
hospital

1920
takes first
airplane ride

1921
earns pilot's
license

Amelia earned her pilot's license in 1921. At age 30, Amelia was the first woman passenger to fly across the Atlantic Ocean.

Amelia looking out from the *Friendship* airplane after flying across the Atlantic Ocean

Time Line

1897	1917	1920	1921
born	works in hospital	takes first airplane ride	earns pilot's license

In 1928, Amelia flew across the United States and back. In 1932, Amelia flew across the Atlantic Ocean. She was the first woman pilot to make these flights alone.

◀ crowds in Ireland greeting Amelia in May 1932

1928
flies alone across
United States

15

Time Line

1897
born

1917
works in
hospital

1920
takes first
airplane ride

1921
earns pilot's
license

In 1935, Amelia became the first pilot to fly alone across the Pacific Ocean. But she had another dream. She wanted to be the first woman to fly around the world.

crowds in California greeting Amelia in January 1935

1928
flies alone across
United States

1935
flies alone across
Pacific Ocean

Time Line

1897	1917	1920	1921
born	works in hospital	takes first airplane ride	earns pilot's license

In 1937, Amelia and navigator Fred Noonan began their trip. They flew most of the way around the world. But their airplane disappeared over the Pacific Ocean.

Amelia and navigator Fred Noonan

1928	1935	1937
flies alone across United States	flies alone across Pacific Ocean	disappears over Pacific Ocean

Time Line

1897	1917	1920	1921
born	works in hospital	takes first airplane ride	earns pilot's license

Amelia, Fred, and their airplane were never found. Their deaths are still a mystery. Amelia Earhart is called the "First Lady of the Air."

1928
flies alone across
United States

1935
flies alone across
Pacific Ocean

1937
disappears over
Pacific Ocean

Words to Know

airfield—a large space that has a runway for airplanes to take off and land

air show—an event where pilots display their flying skills

Atlantic Ocean—the large body of salt water east of North America

disappear—to go out of sight or to go missing

explore—to travel to find out what a place is like

license—an official paper that gives a person permission to do something or to own something

mystery—something that is hard to explain or understand

navigator—a person who uses maps, compasses, and the stars to guide an airplane or ship

Pacific Ocean—the large body of salt water west of North America

pilot—a person who flies an airplane

Read More

Devillier, Christy. *Amelia Earhart.* First Biographies. Edina, Minn.: Abdo, 2001.

Raatma, Lucia. *Amelia Earhart.* Trailblazers of the Modern World. Milwaukee: World Almanac Library, 2001.

Rosenthal, Marilyn, and Daniel Freeman. *Amelia Earhart: A Photo-Illustrated Biography.* Mankato, Minn.: Bridgestone Books, 1999.

Internet Sites

Amelia Earhart
http://www.ameliaearhart.com

Amelia Earhart
http://www.americaslibrary.gov/cgi-bin/page.cgi/aa/earhart

Amelia Earhart Birthplace Museum
http://www.ameliaearhartmuseum.org

National Aviation Hall of Fame: Amelia Earhart Putnam
http://www.nationalaviation.org/enshrinee/putnam.html

Index/Word List

Word Count: 218
Early-Intervention Level: 22

Editorial Credits
Martha E. H. Rustad, editor; Heather Kindseth, series designer; Linda Clavel, illustrator; Patrick D. Dentinger, book designer; Wanda Winch, photo researcher; Karen Risch, product planning editor

Photo Credits
Associated Press, cover
Atchison County, Kansas, Historical Society, 6
Brown Brothers, Sterling, PA, 8
Corbis, 16
Corbis/Bettmann, 1, 4, 14, 18
Hulton/Archive by Getty Images, 10, 12, 20